I Love My Pet

IGUANA

Aaron Carr

LET'S READ

AV2 BY WEIGL™

ADDED VALUE • AUDIO VISUAL

www.av2books.com

LET'S READ
AV²
BY WEIGL™
ADDED VALUE • AUDIO VISUAL

Go to **www.av2books.com**, and enter this book's unique code.

BOOK CODE

Q670296

AV² by Weigl brings you media enhanced books that support active learning.

AV² provides enriched content that supplements and complements this book. Weigl's AV² books strive to create inspired learning and engage young minds in a total learning experience.

Your AV² Media Enhanced books come alive with...

Audio
Listen to sections of the book read aloud.

Video
Watch informative video clips.

Embedded Weblinks
Gain additional information for research.

Try This!
Complete activities and hands-on experiments.

Key Words
Study vocabulary, and complete a matching word activity.

Quizzes
Test your knowledge.

Slide Show
View images and captions, and prepare a presentation.

... and much, much more!

Published by AV² by Weigl
350 5th Avenue, 59th Floor New York, NY 10118
Website: www.av2books.com www.weigl.com

Library of Congress Cataloguing in Publication data available upon request.
Fax 1-866-449-3445 for the attention of the Publishing Records department.

ISBN 978-1-62127-295-3 (hardcover)
ISBN 978-1-62127-302-8 (softcover)

Printed in the United States of America in North Mankato, Minnesota
1 2 3 4 5 6 7 8 9 0 16 15 14 13 12

122012
WEP301112

Senior Editor: Aaron Carr   Art Director: Terry Paulhus

Weigl acknowledges Getty Images as the primary image supplier for this title.

I Love My Pet

IGUANA

CONTENTS

I love my pet iguana.
I take good care of him.

4

My pet iguana hatched from an egg. He could crawl around right after hatching.

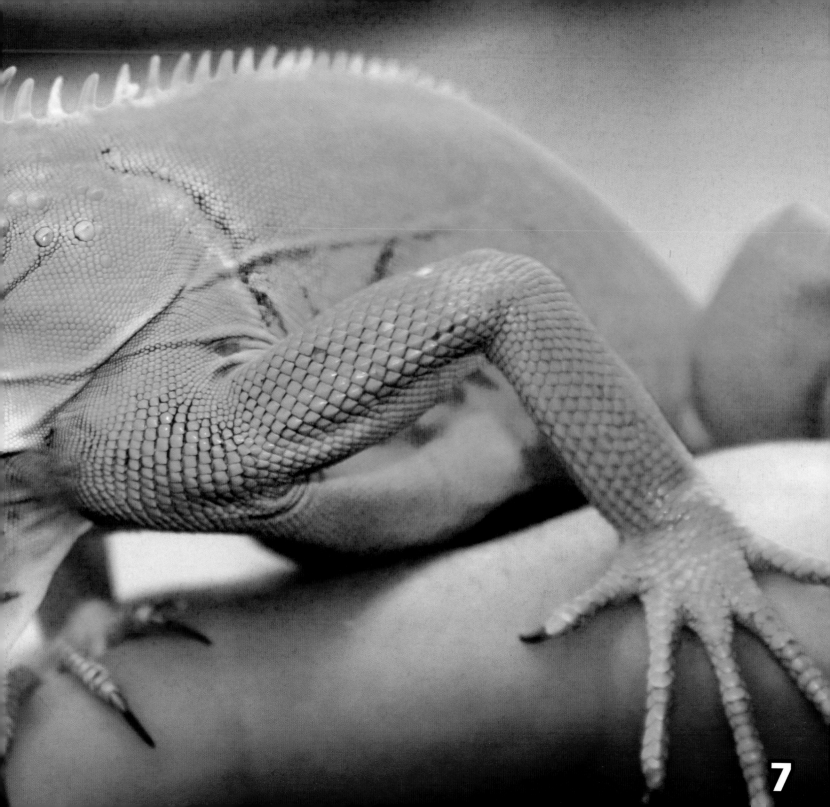

My pet iguana was three months old
when I brought him home.
He was full grown by three years old.

Iguanas can grow
up to 7 feet long.

My pet iguana has three eyes.
He has an eye
on each side of his head.
He also has a third eye
on the top of his head.

My pet iguana has a very long tail. His tail may be three times longer than his body.

An iguana can drop and regrow its tail.

13

My pet iguana is cold blooded. He needs lights in his cage to keep him warm.

My pet iguana eats fruits
and other plants.
He likes to eat flowers.

Iguanas stop
eating when they are sick.

My pet iguana
needs a lot of care.
He needs to be fed,
washed, and played with
every day.

19

I help make sure
my pet iguana is healthy.
I love my pet iguana.

IGUANA FACTS

These pages provide more detail about the interesting facts found in the book. They are intended to be used by adults as a learning support to help young readers round out their knowledge of each animal featured in the *I Love My Pet* series.

Pages 4–5

I love my pet iguana. I take good care of him. There are about 30 kinds of iguanas. Most people keep green iguanas as pets. They are great pets when properly cared for. To stay healthy and happy, iguanas need a clean cage, food, water, and exercise. They also need plenty of light, heat, and space. Each iguana is different, however, and owners need to learn their iguana's likes and dislikes.

Pages 6–7

My pet iguana hatched from an egg. He could crawl around right after hatching. Iguanas are reptiles. Reptiles lay eggs to have babies. When iguanas hatch from their eggs, they are called hatchlings. Hatchlings use a small claw on their nose, called an egg tooth, to break out of their eggs. Iguana hatchlings move around and find their own food right away after birth.

Pages 8–9

My pet iguana was three months old when I brought him home. He was full grown by three years of age. Most iguanas are ready to live with their new owners by three to five months old. They are about 1 foot (0.3 m) long at this age. Iguanas reach full size after three or four years. They can grow up to 6.5 feet (2 m) long and weigh 20 pounds (9.1 kilograms).

Pages 10–11

My pet iguana has three eyes. He has an eye on each side of his head. He also has a third eye on the top of his head. Iguanas have good eyesight from their two main eyes. They can see in color, which helps them find food. The third eye, called a parietal eye, is a scale on the top of the head. This scale can sense changes in light and dark, but it cannot form images. It helps iguanas avoid predators.

My pet iguana has a very long tail. His tail may be three times longer than his body. A 6-foot (1.8-m) long iguana could have a 4.5-foot (1.4 m) long tail. The iguana uses this long tail to keep its balance. The iguana also uses its tail to protect itself from other animals. If a predator grabs an iguana's tail, the iguana can break off its tail and escape. The iguana then grows a new tail.

My pet iguana is cold blooded. He needs lights in his cage to keep him warm. As a cold blooded animal, iguanas cannot make their own heat to stay warm. Instead, iguanas must sit in sunlight to warm up or dip into water to cool off. A pet iguana needs special heat lights in its cage. Iguanas also need moisture. They should spend about 20 to 30 minutes in water each week.

My pet iguana eats fruits and other plants. He likes to eat flowers. Iguanas are herbivores, or plant eaters. Fruits, vegetables, and flowers are some of the iguana's favorite foods. Pet iguanas should eat a mixture of store-bought and fresh food. Store-bought iguana food should only make up about half of the iguana's diet.

My pet iguana needs a lot of care. He needs to be fed, washed, and played with every day. How much iguanas eat depends on their size. Full-grown iguanas need to be fed two or three times a week. Iguanas do not chew food, so their food needs to be cut into small pieces. If an iguana stops eating, it may be sick. It will need to be taken to a veterinarian right away.

I help make sure my pet iguana is healthy. I love my pet iguana. Keeping an iguana healthy and happy is a big job. They need to be bathed every day. Pet owners also need to give their iguana food and water every day. The cage must also be cleaned daily. Taking time every day to play with the iguana and give it exercise is also important to the animal's health.

KEY WORDS

Research has shown that as much as 65 percent of all written material published in English is made up of 300 words. These 300 words cannot be taught using pictures or learned by sounding them out. They must be recognized by sight. This book contains 61 common sight words to help young readers improve their reading fluency and comprehension. This book also teaches young readers several important content words, such as proper nouns. These words are paired with pictures to aid in learning and improve understanding.

Page	Sight Words First Appearance
4	good, him, I, my, of, take
6	after, an, around, could, from, he, right
9	by, can, feet, grown, home, long, old, three, to, up, was, when, years
11	a, also, each, eyes, has, head, his, on, side, the
12	and, be, its, may, than, times, very
15	in, is, keep, lights, needs
16	are, eats, likes, other, plants, stop, they
18	day, every, played, with
21	help, make

Page	Content Words First Appearance
4	iguana, pet
6	egg
9	months
11	top
12	body, tail
15	cage
16	flowers, fruits, sick
18	care
21	healthy

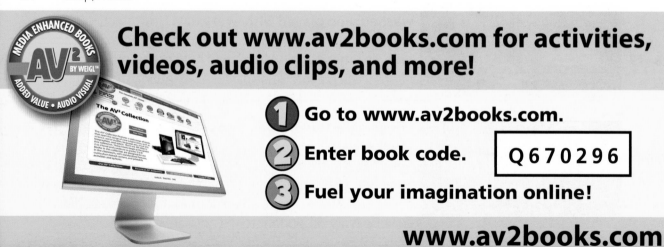

Check out www.av2books.com for activities, videos, audio clips, and more!

1 Go to www.av2books.com.

2 Enter book code. Q670296

3 Fuel your imagination online!

www.av2books.com